Doodle Dazzles
Adult Coloring Book

Suzanne "Robbie" Hay

authorHOUSE®

AuthorHouse™
1663 Liberty Drive
Bloomington, IN 47403
www.authorhouse.com
Phone: 1 (800) 839-8640

Published by AuthorHouse 02/19/2016

ISBN: 978-1-5049-8102-6 (sc)
ISBN: 978-1-5049-8103-3 (e)

Adult Coloring Book

Doodle Dazzles

By Robbie Hay

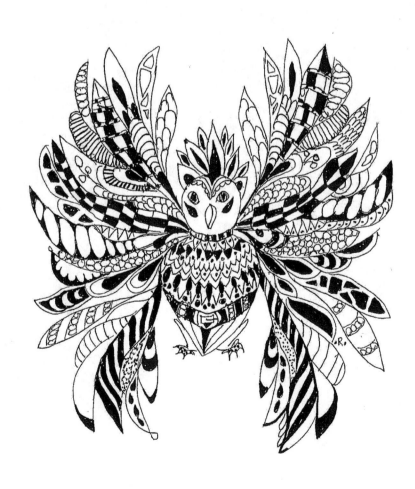

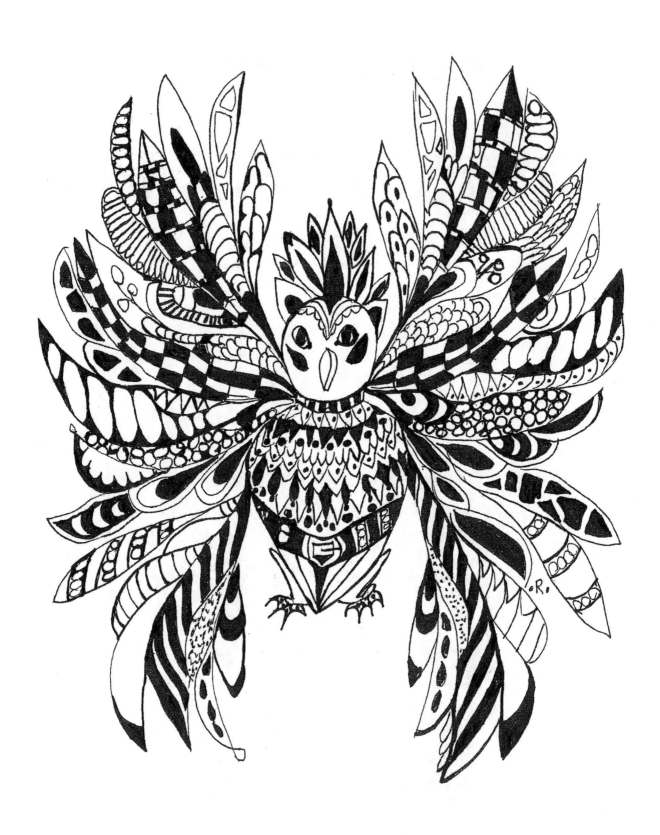

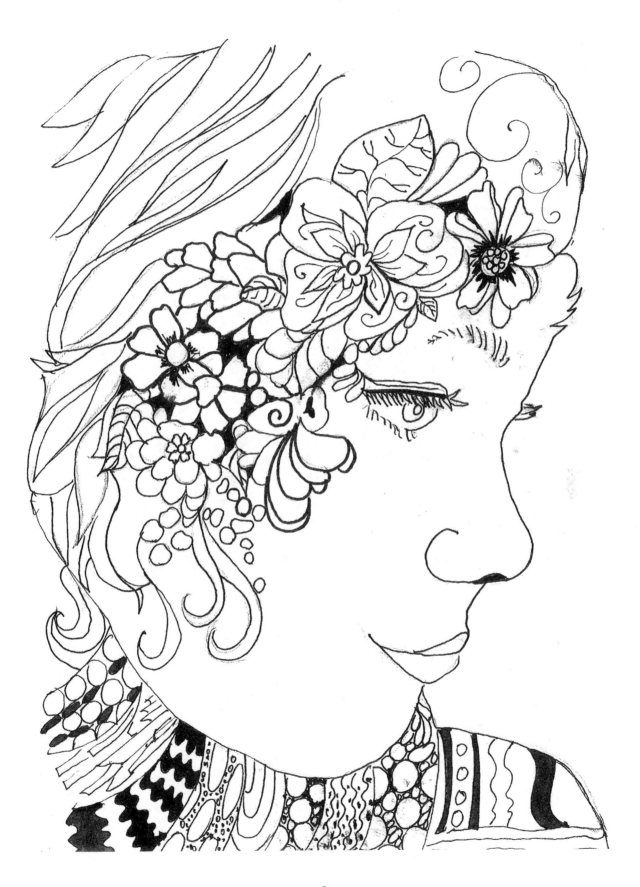

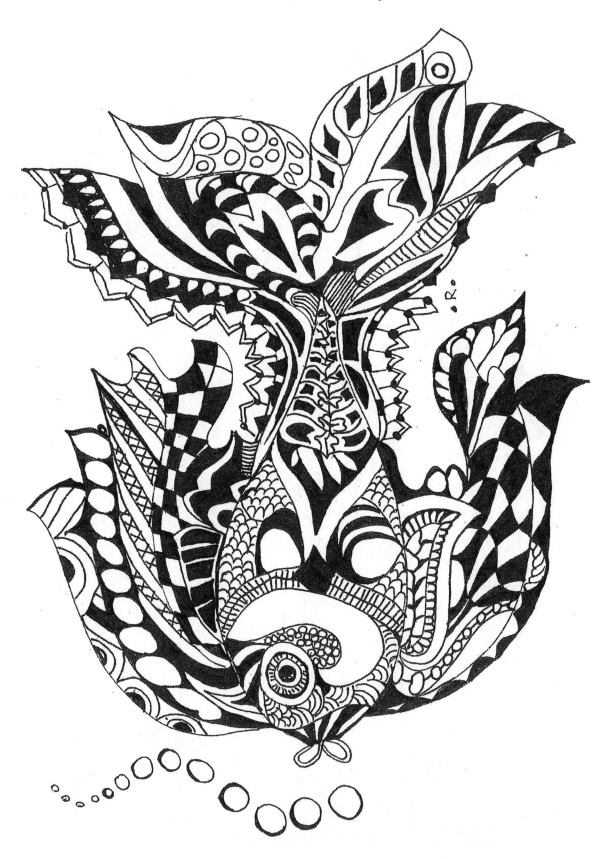

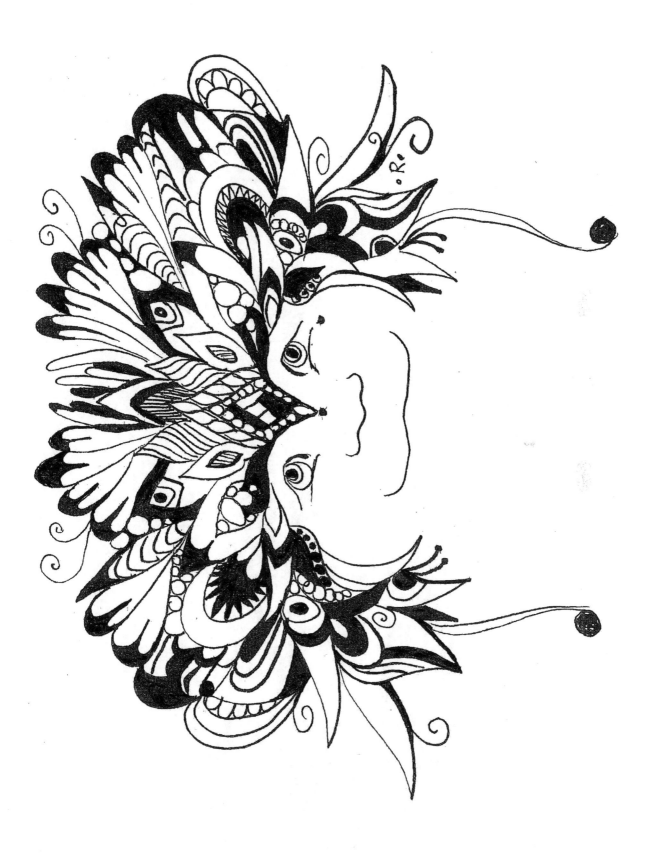

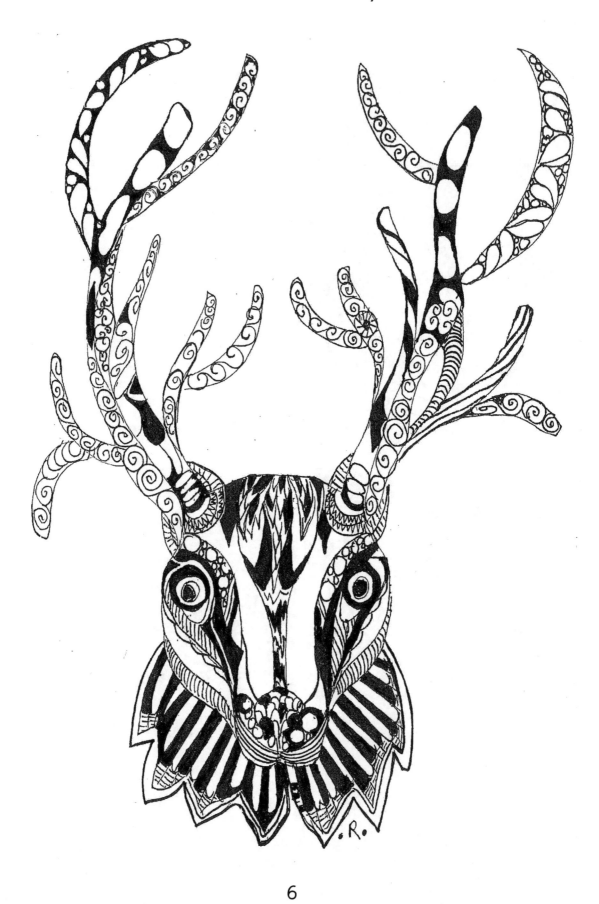

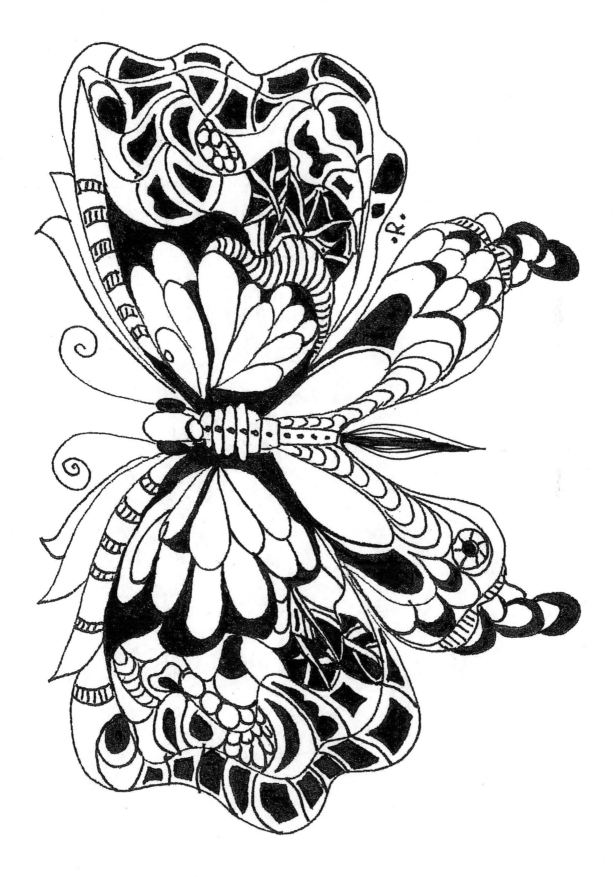

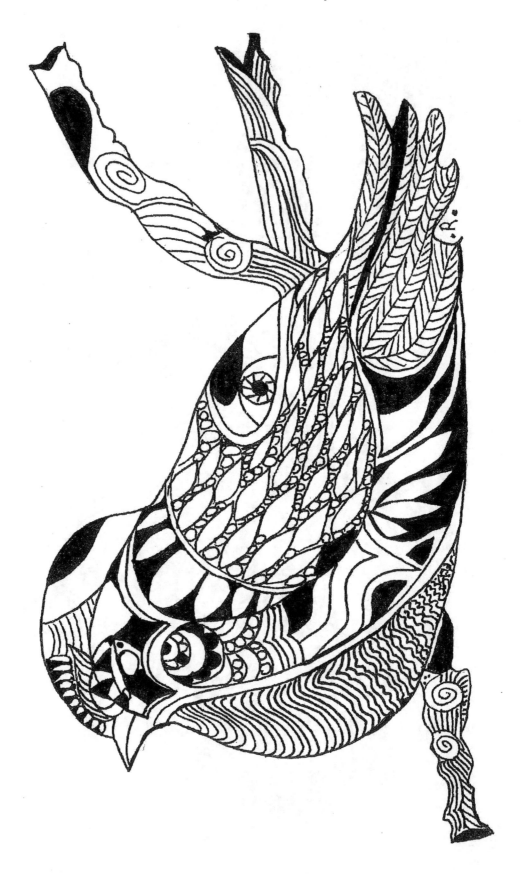

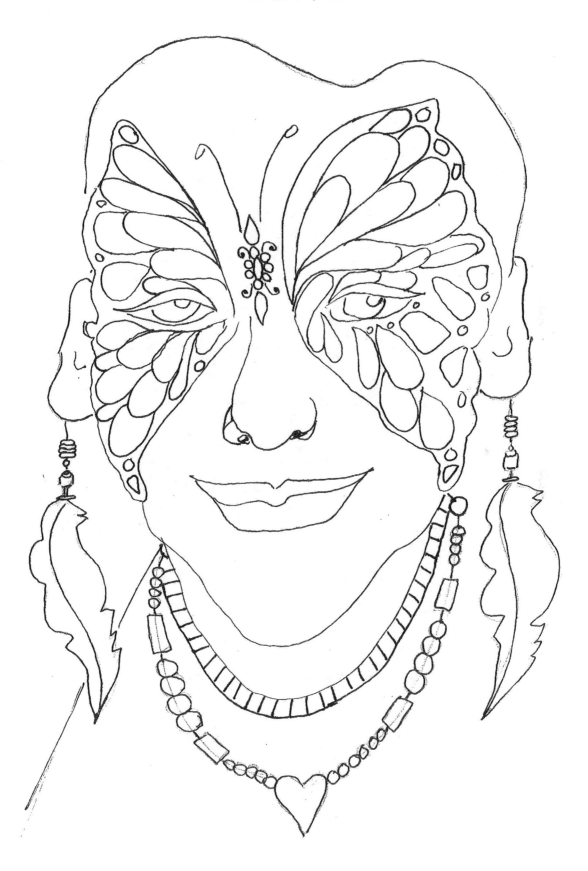

Suzanne "Robbie" Hay

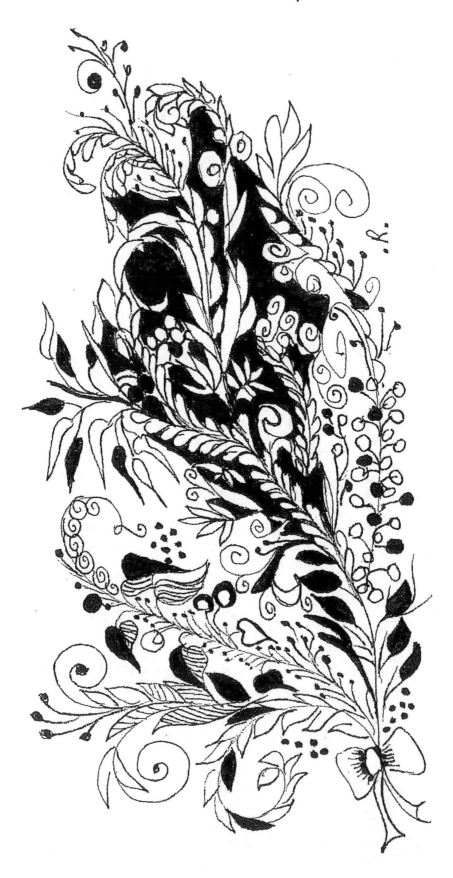

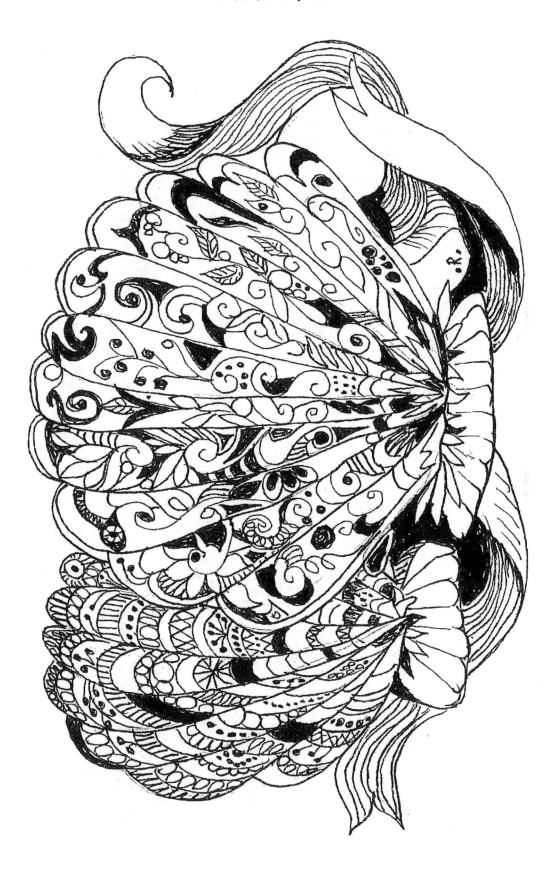

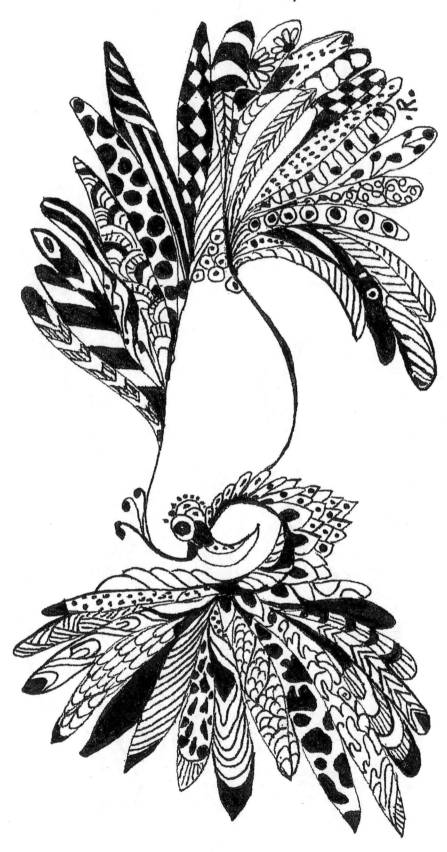

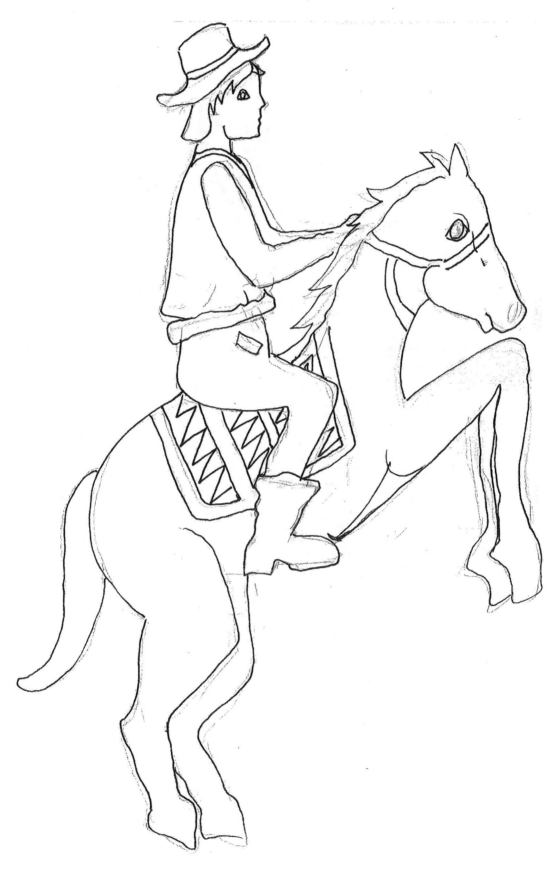

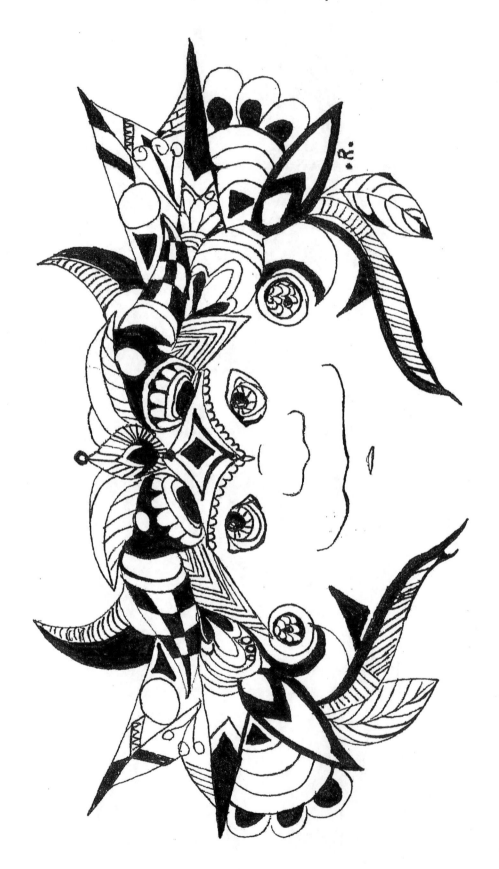

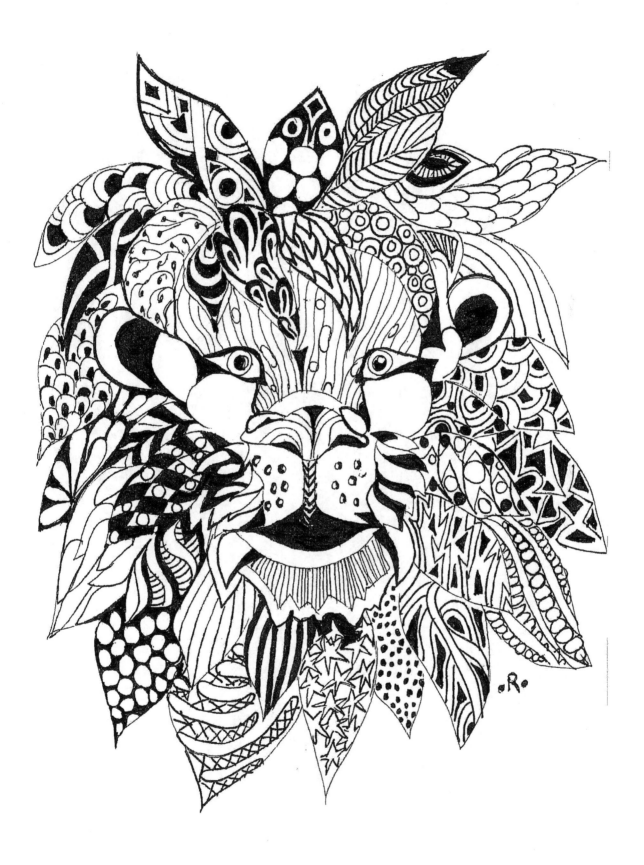

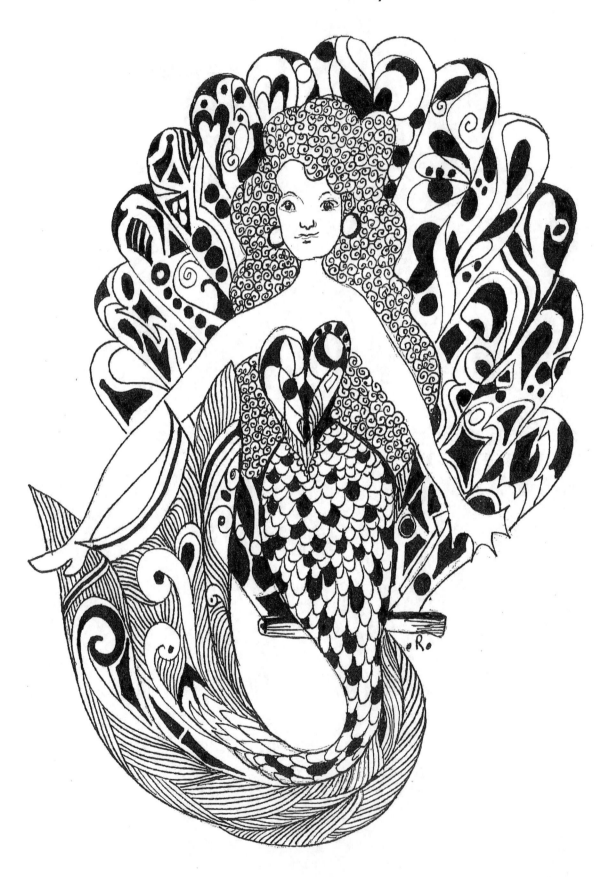

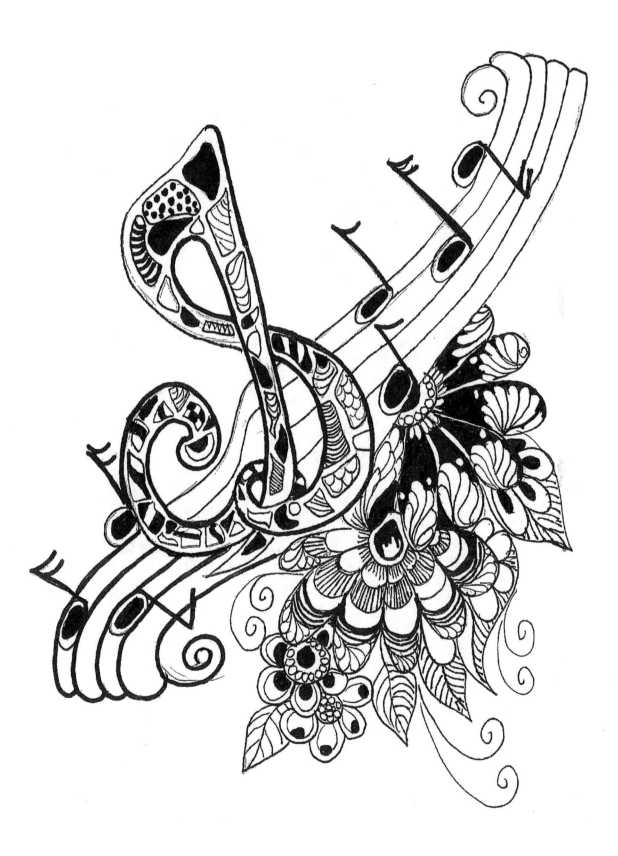

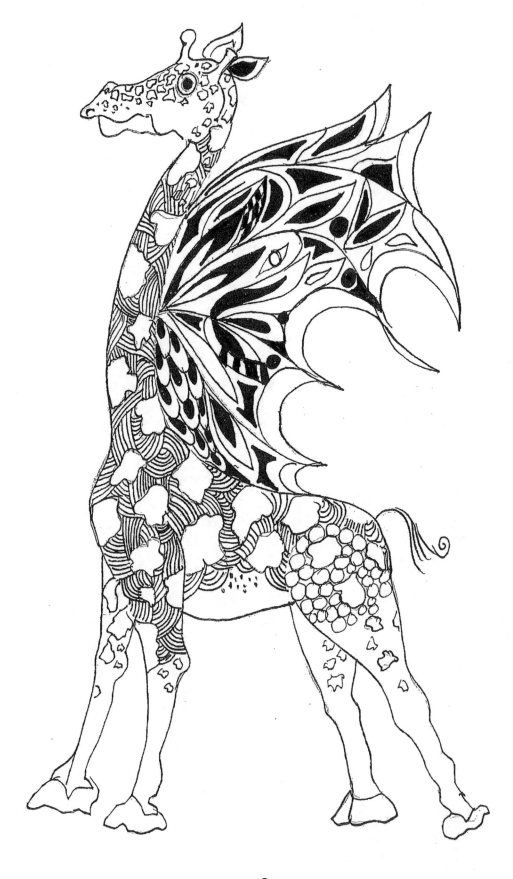

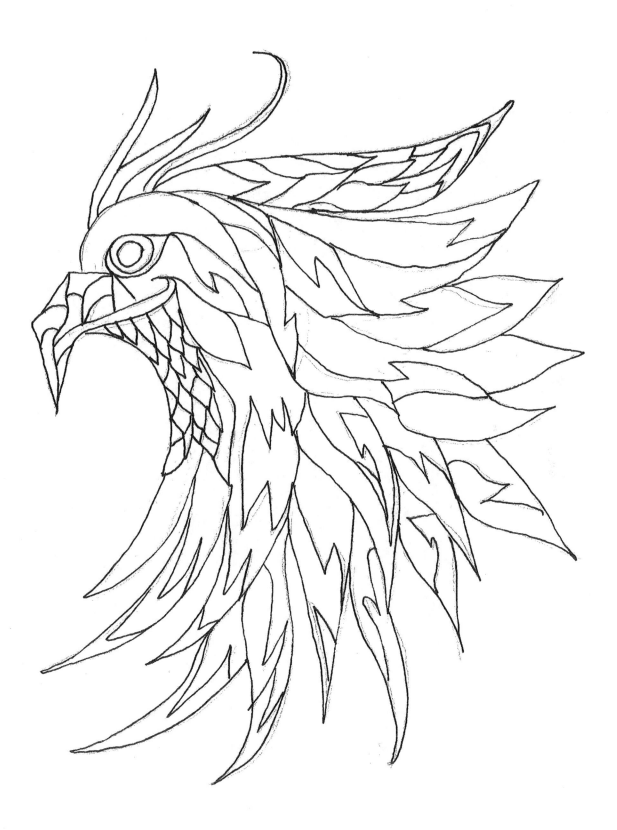

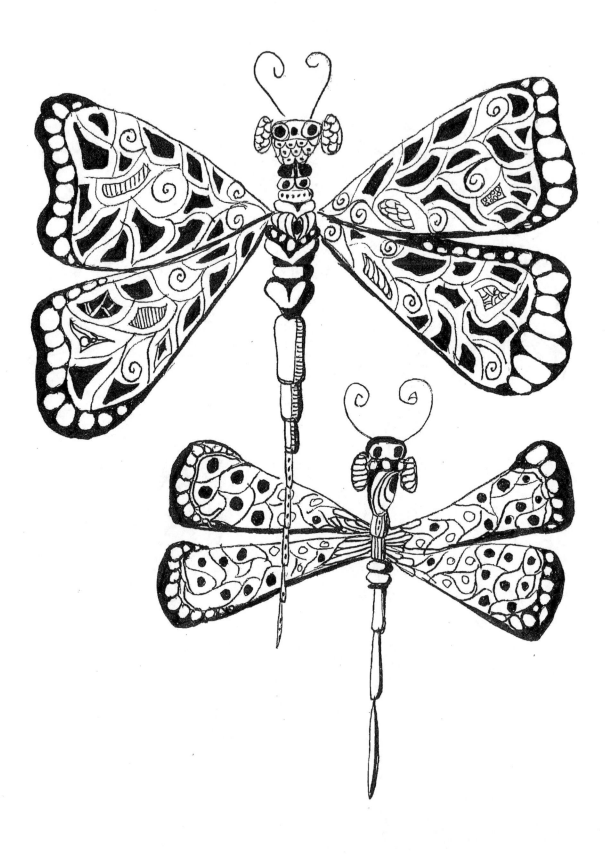

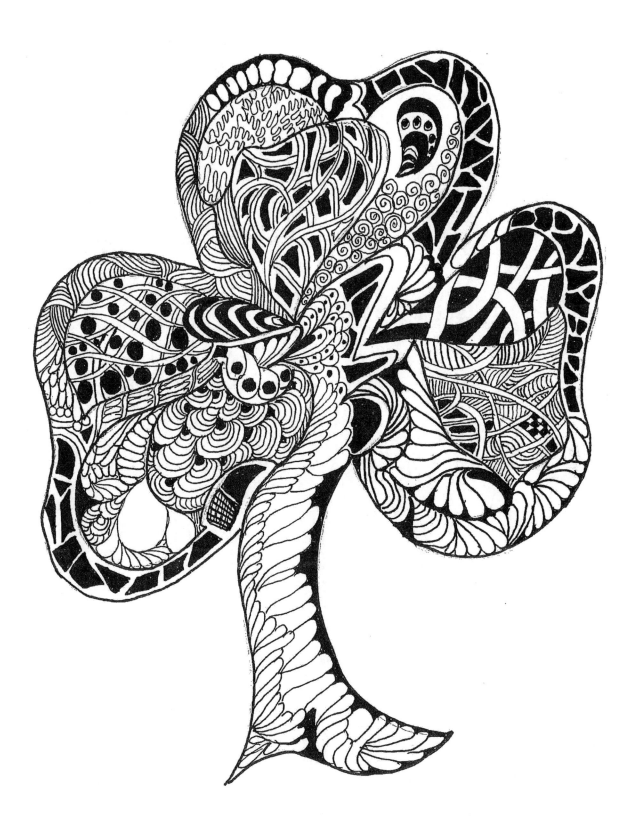

Suzanne "Robbie" Hay

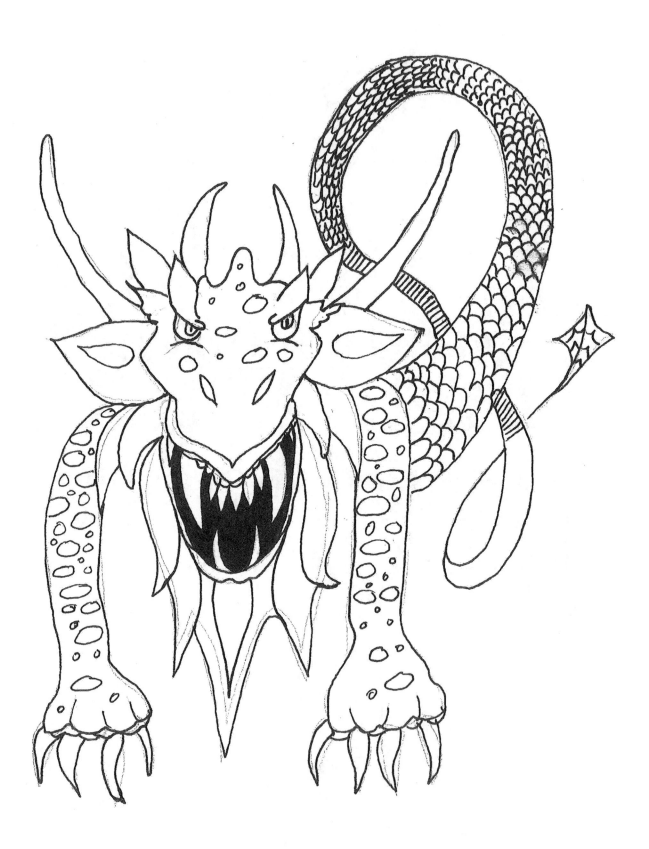

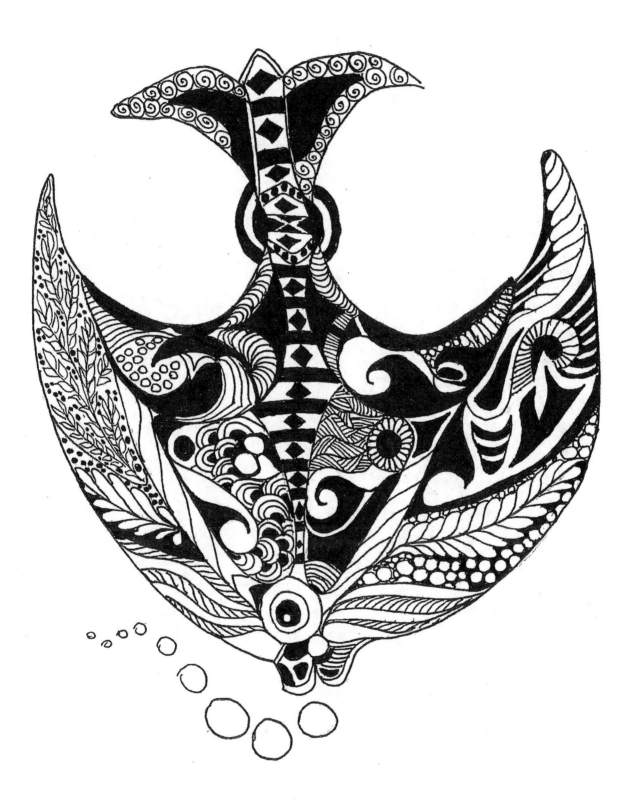

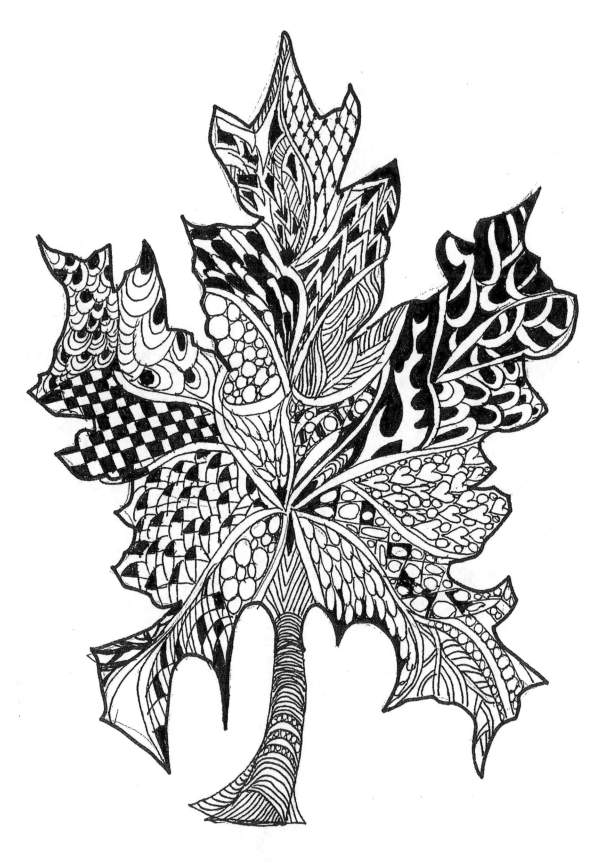

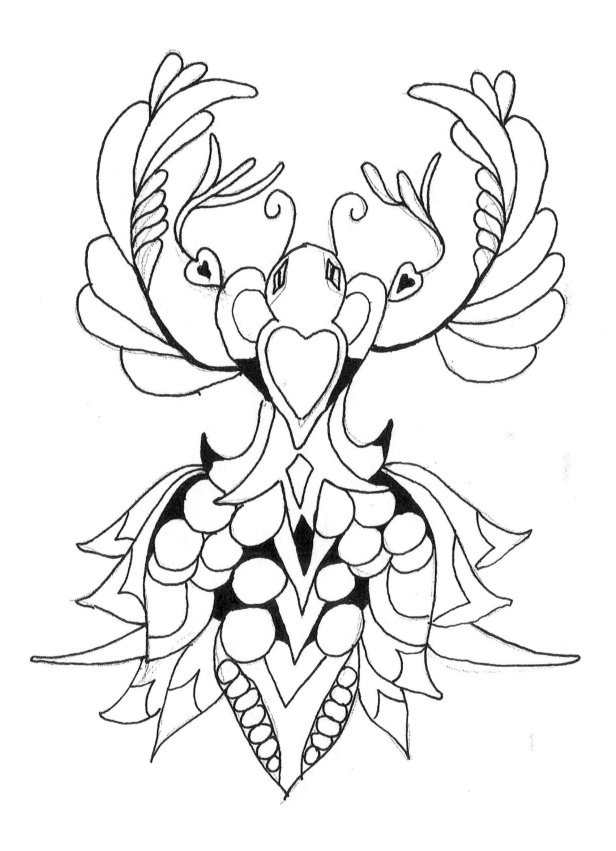

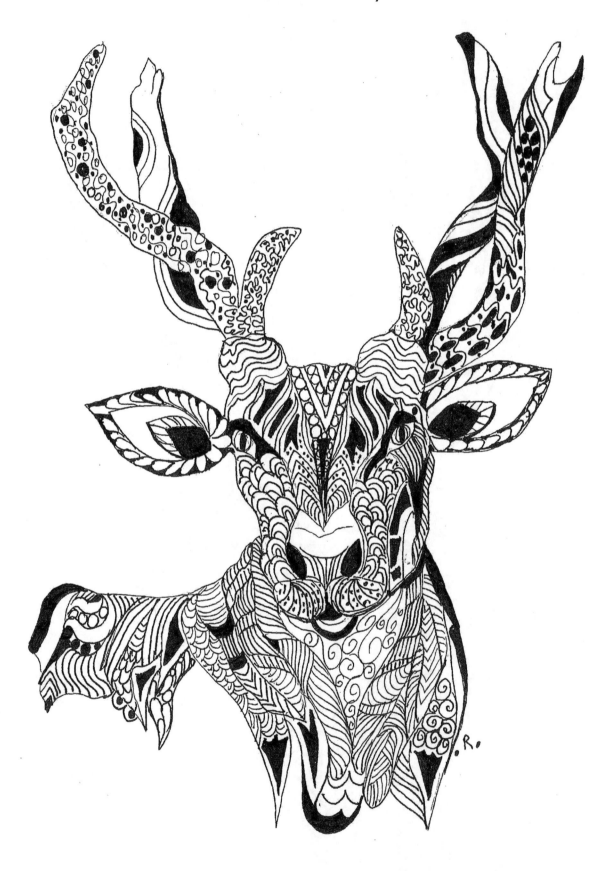

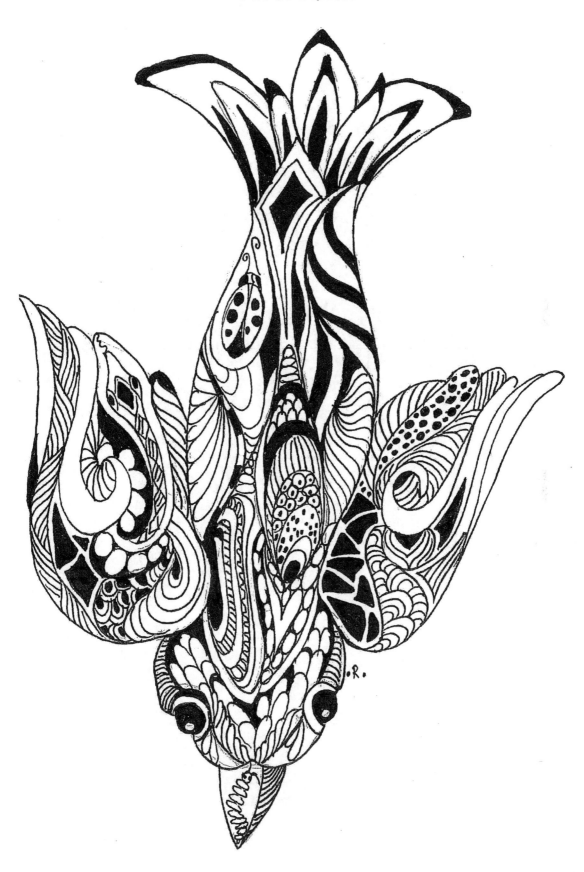

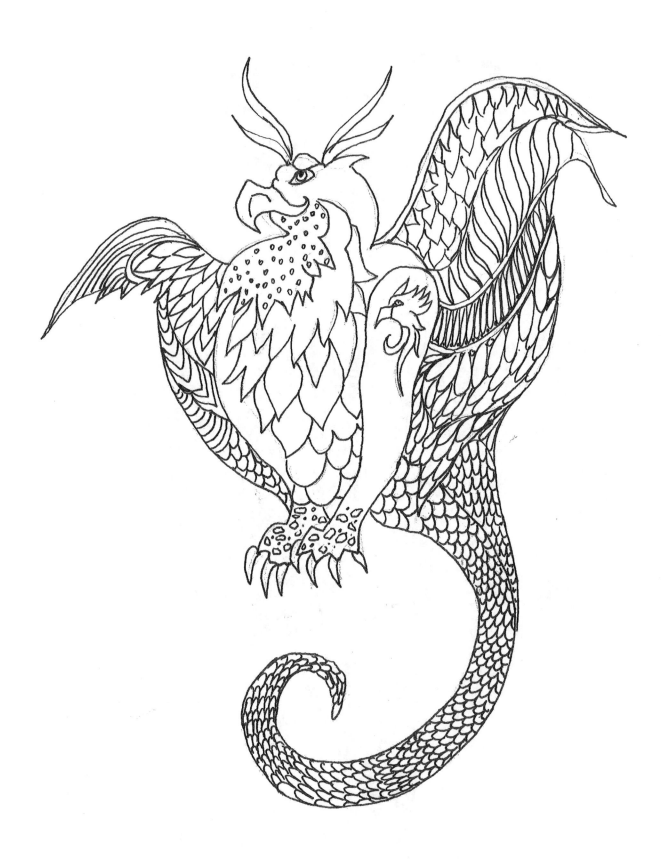

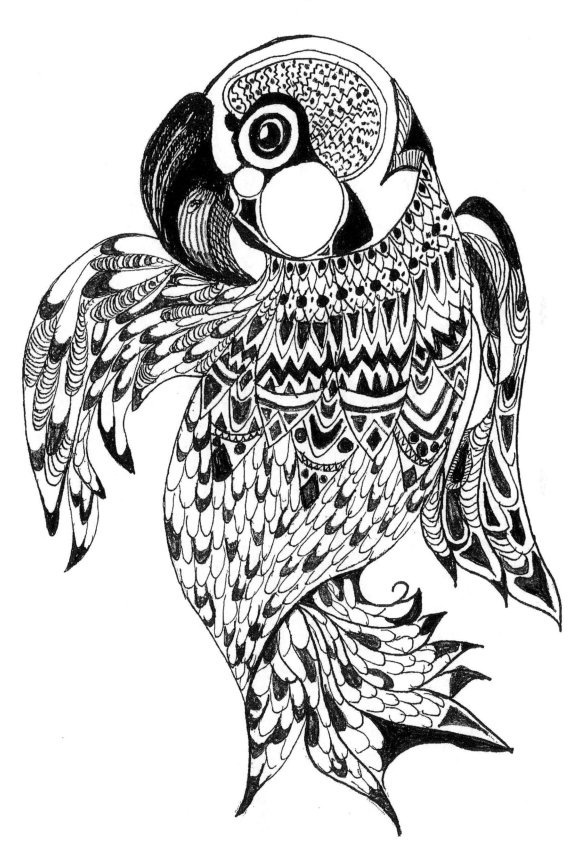

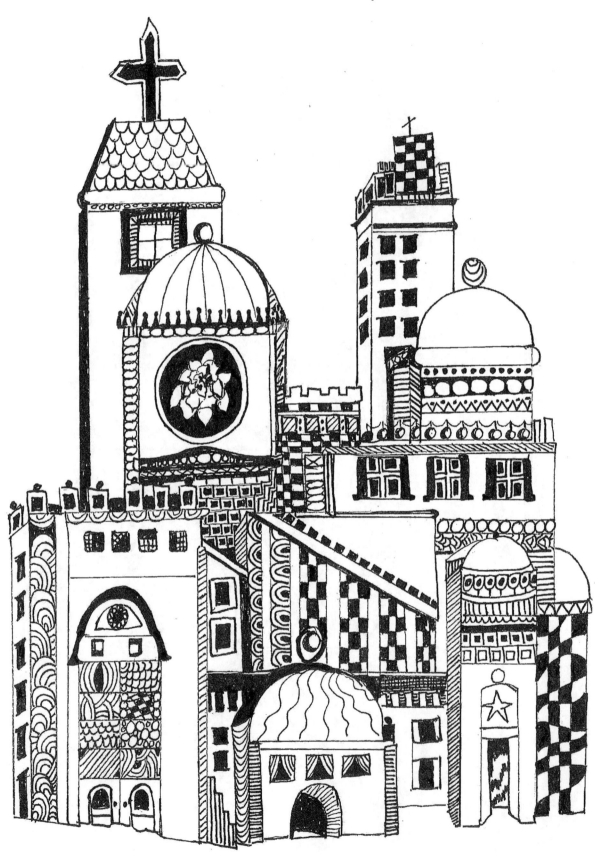

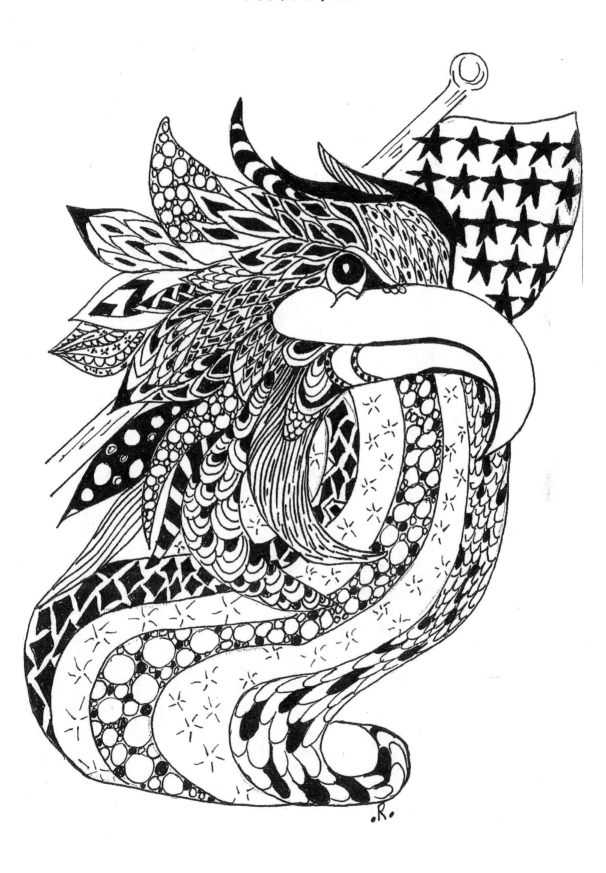

Suzanne "Robbie" Hay

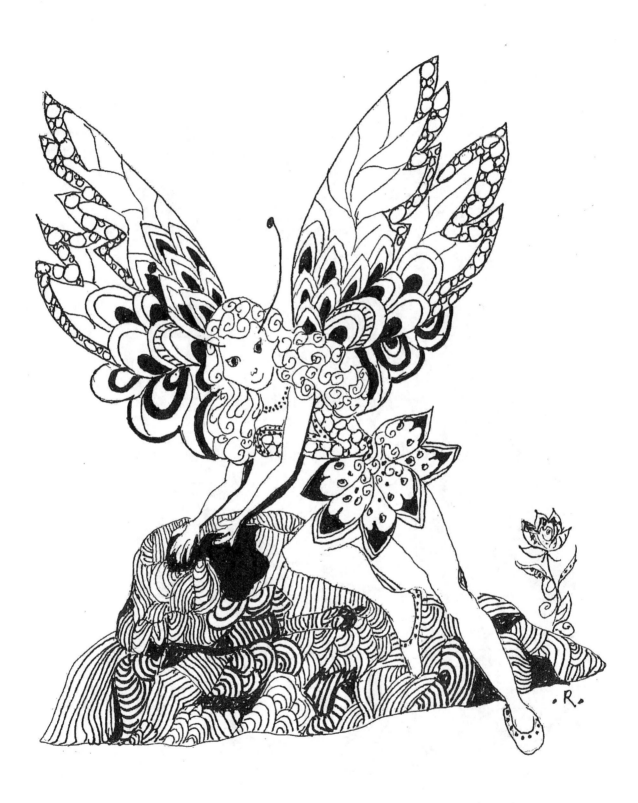

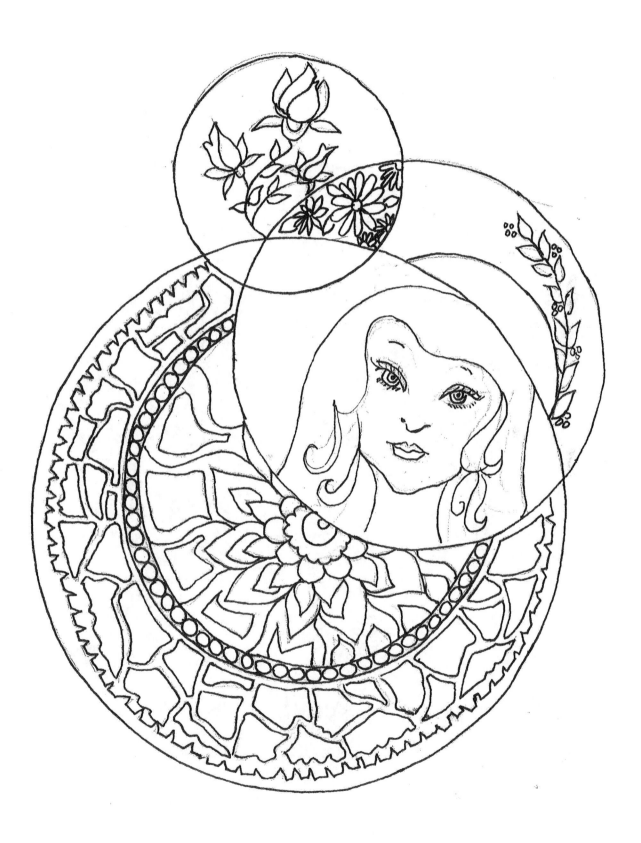

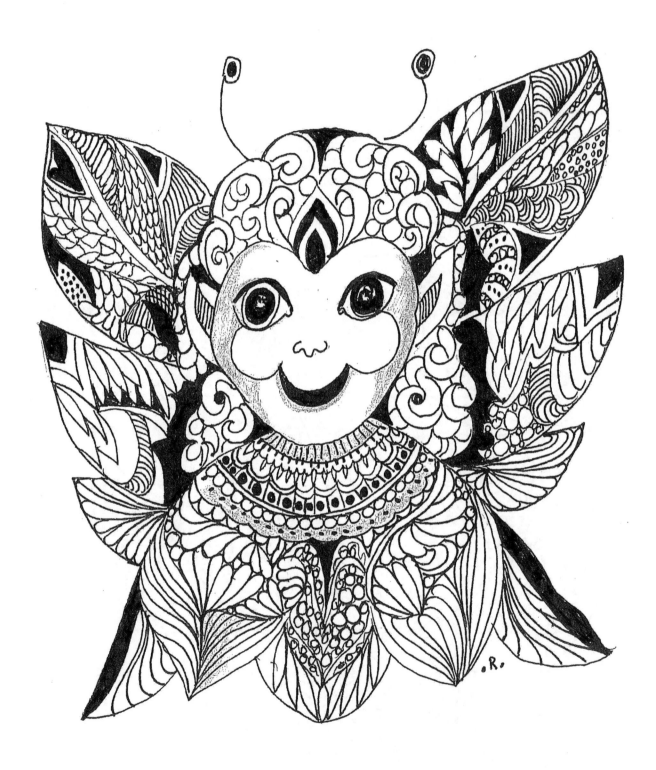

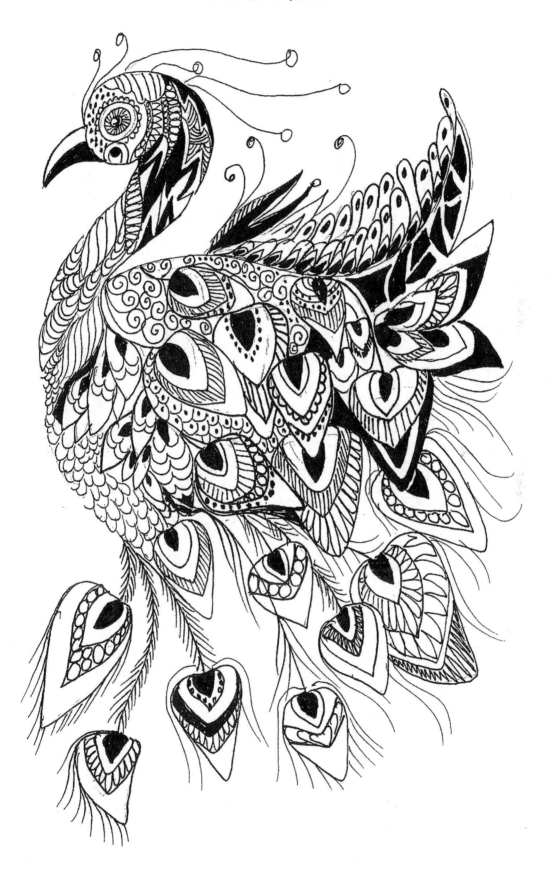

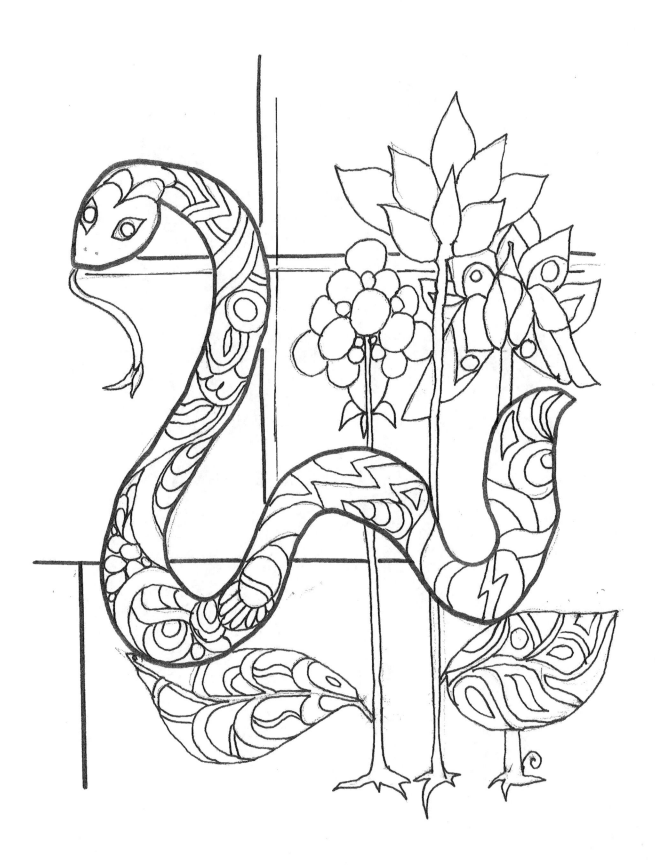

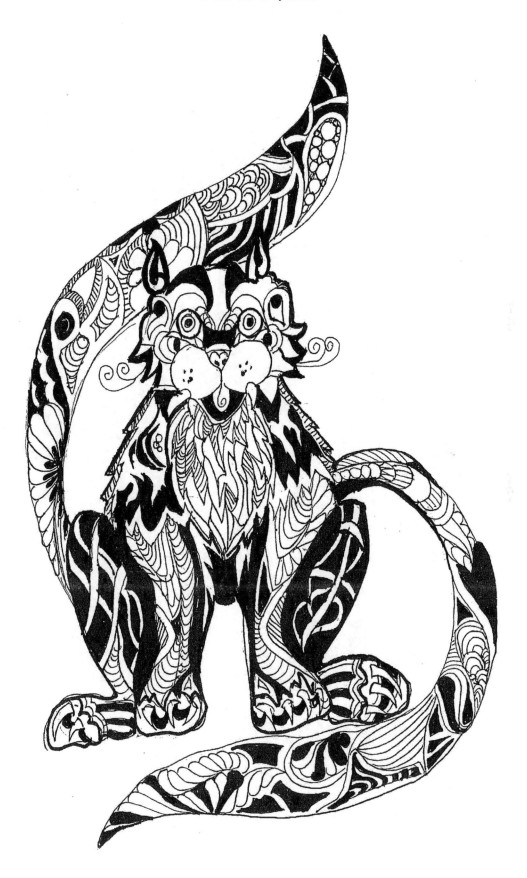

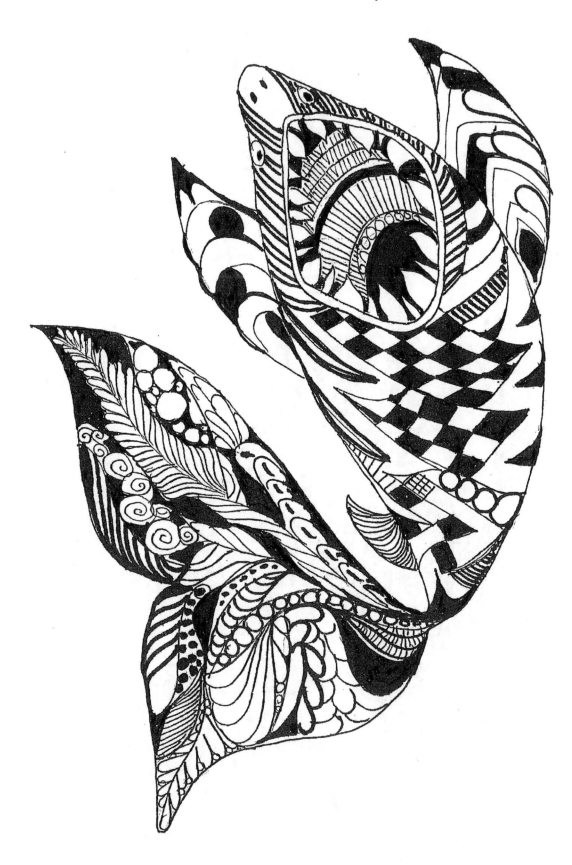

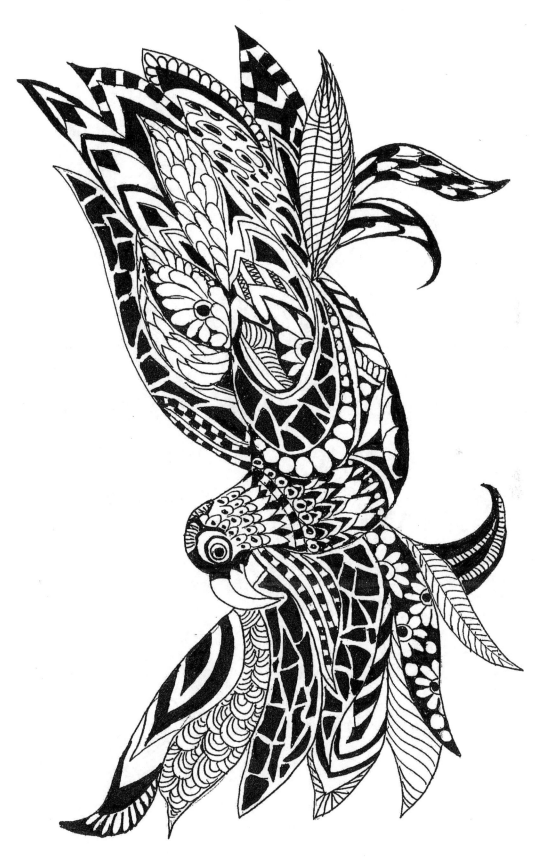

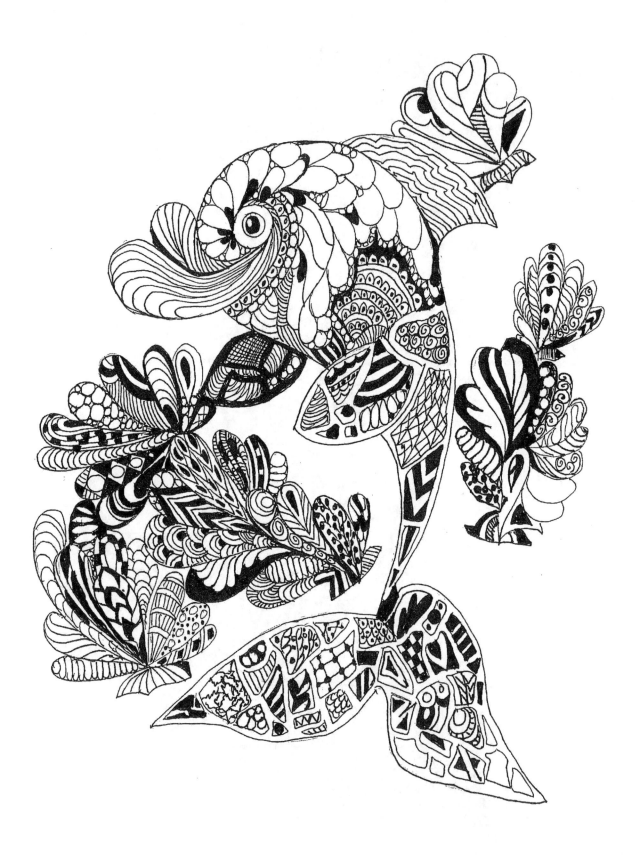

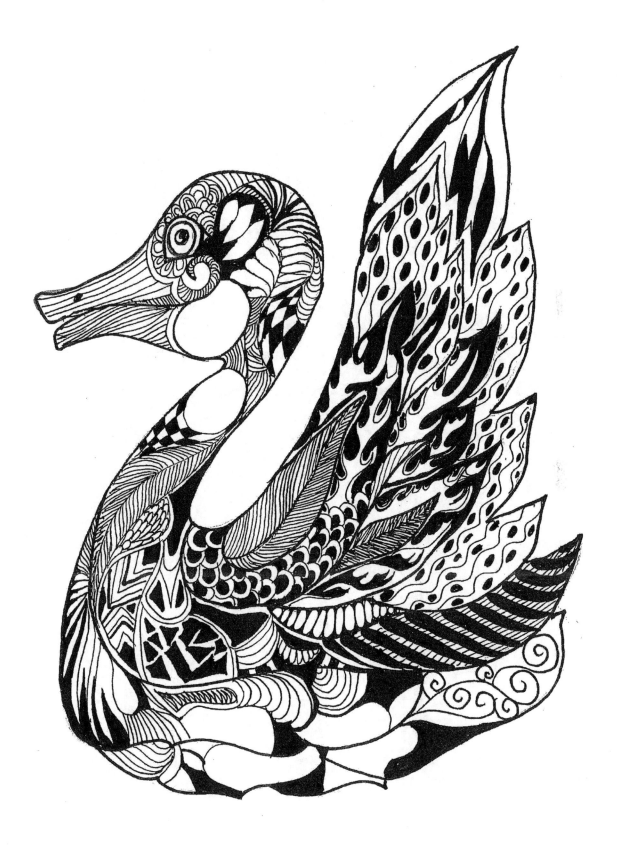

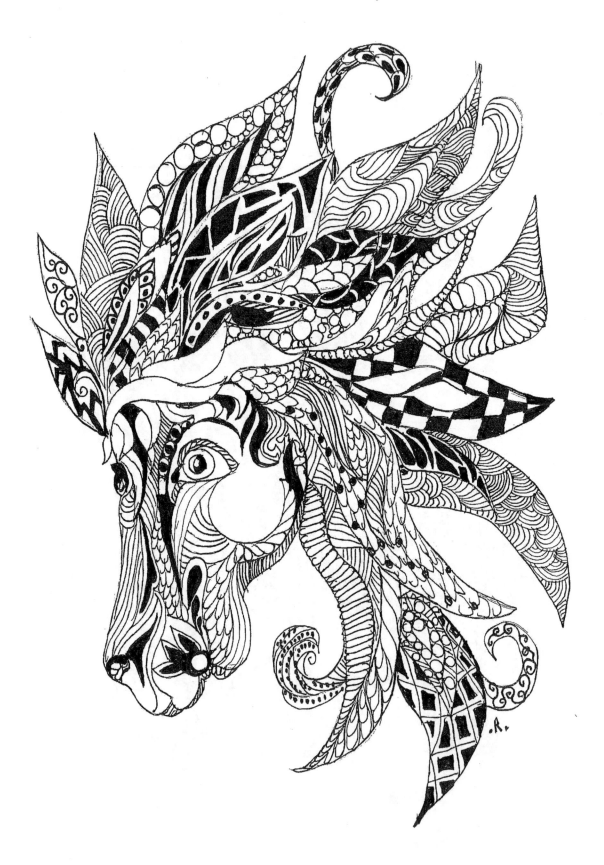

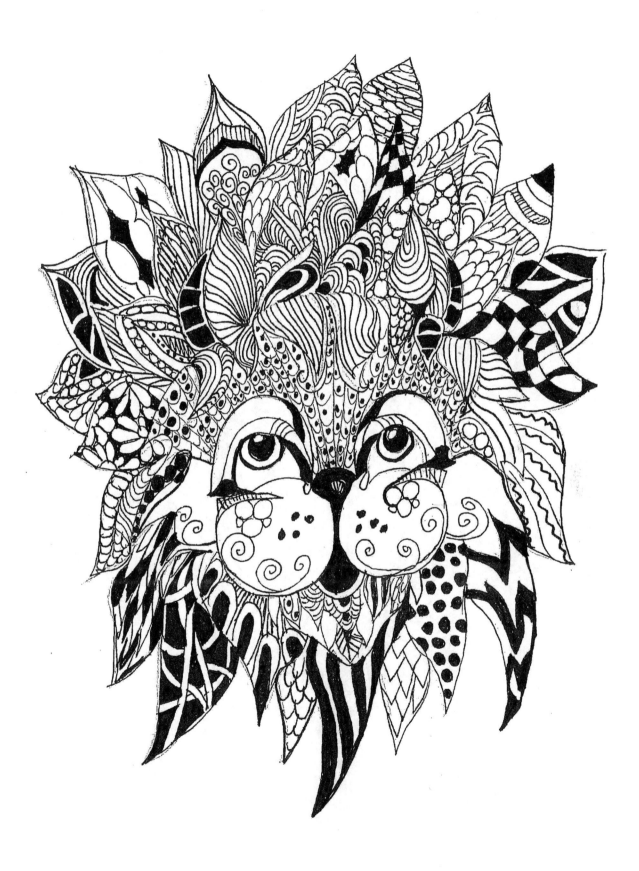

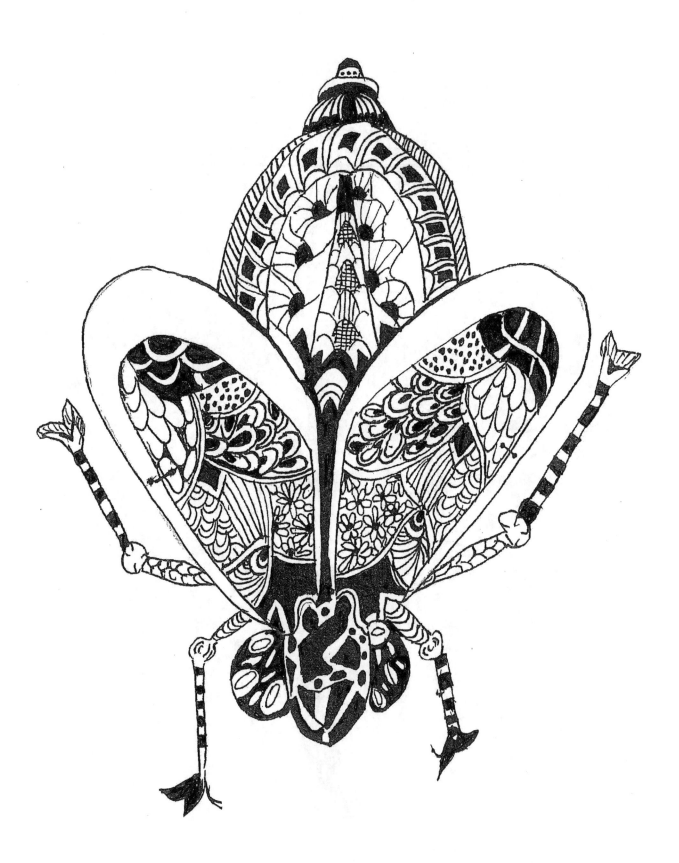

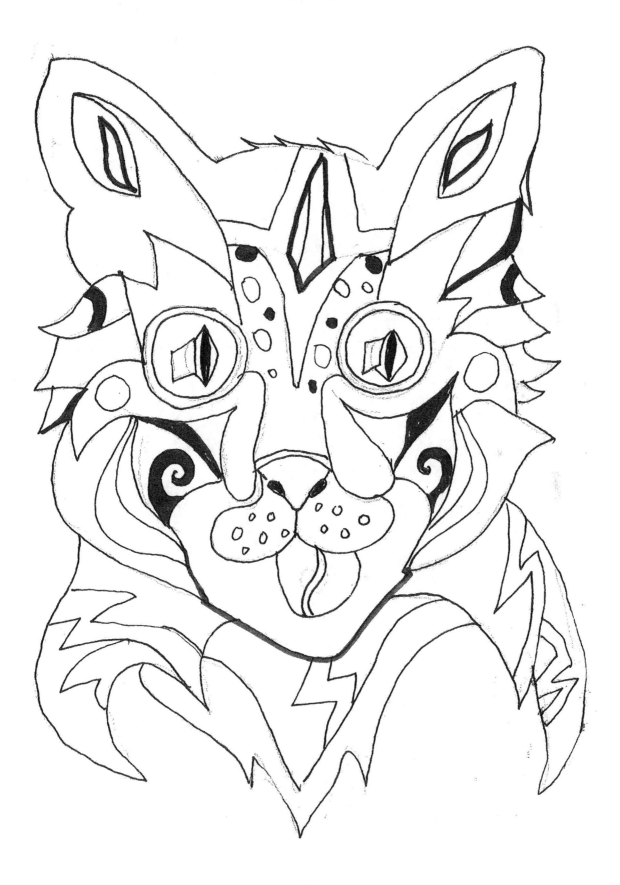

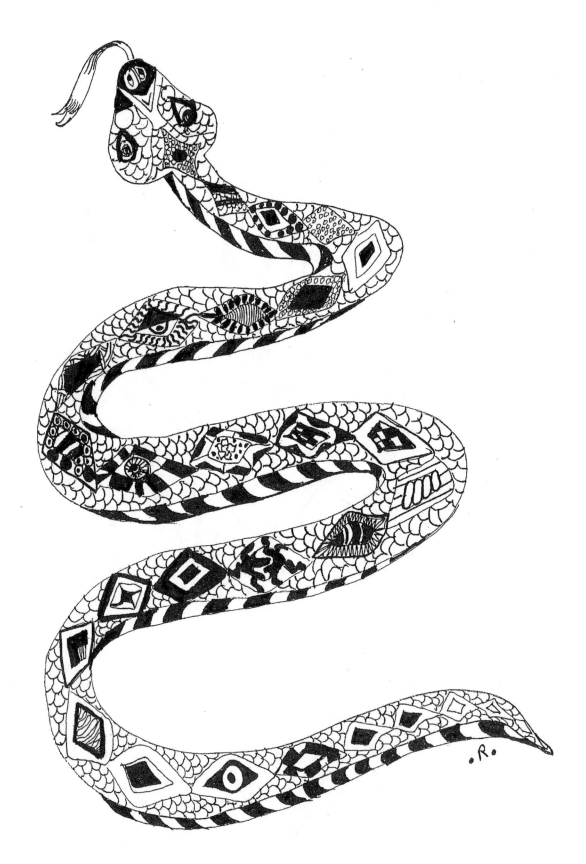

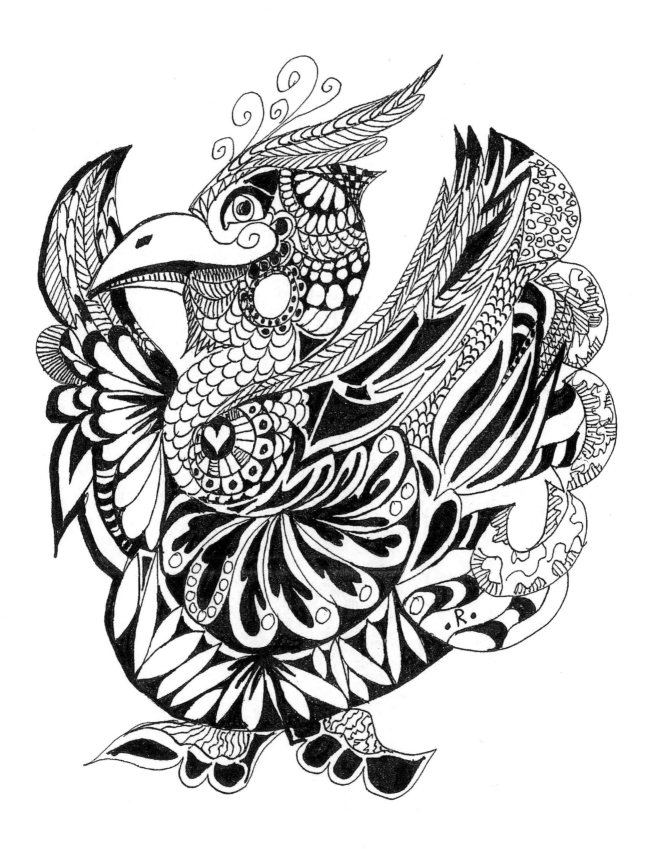

Suzanne "Robbie" Hay

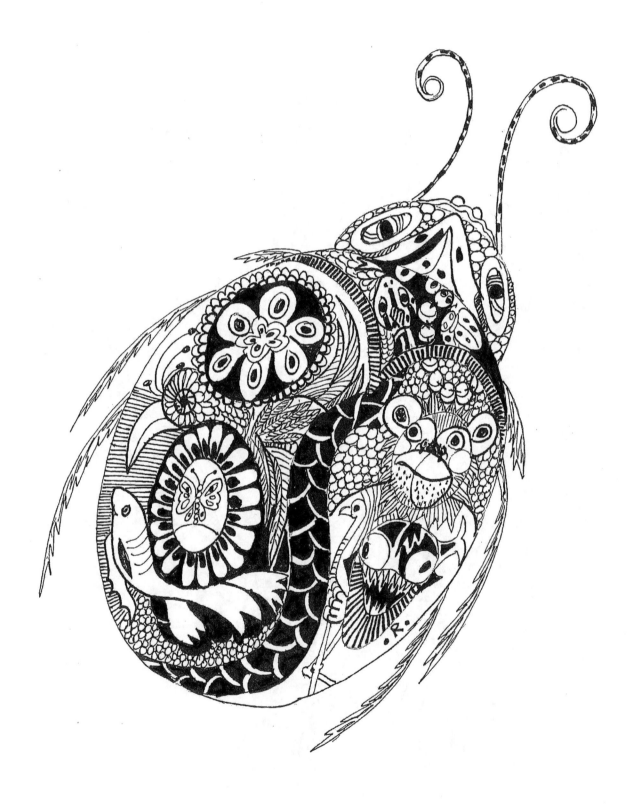

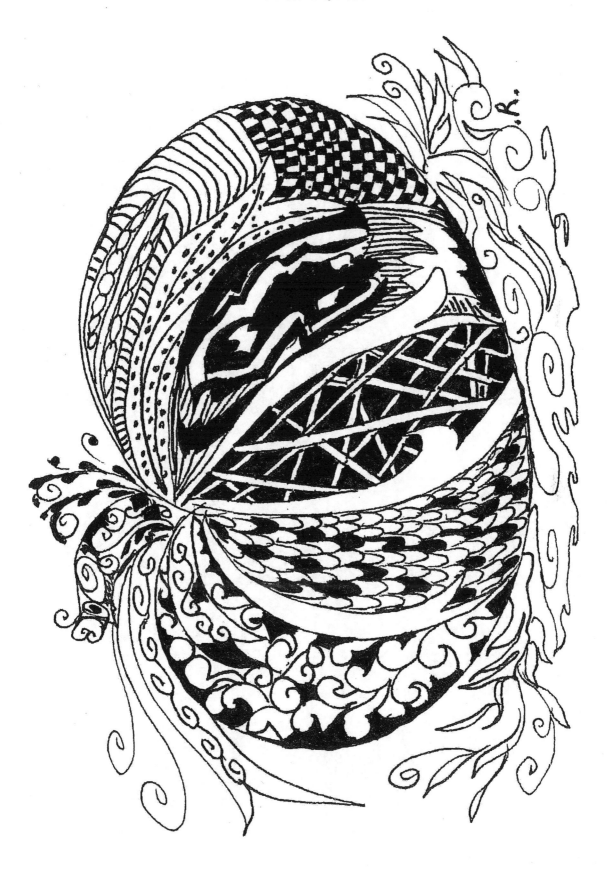

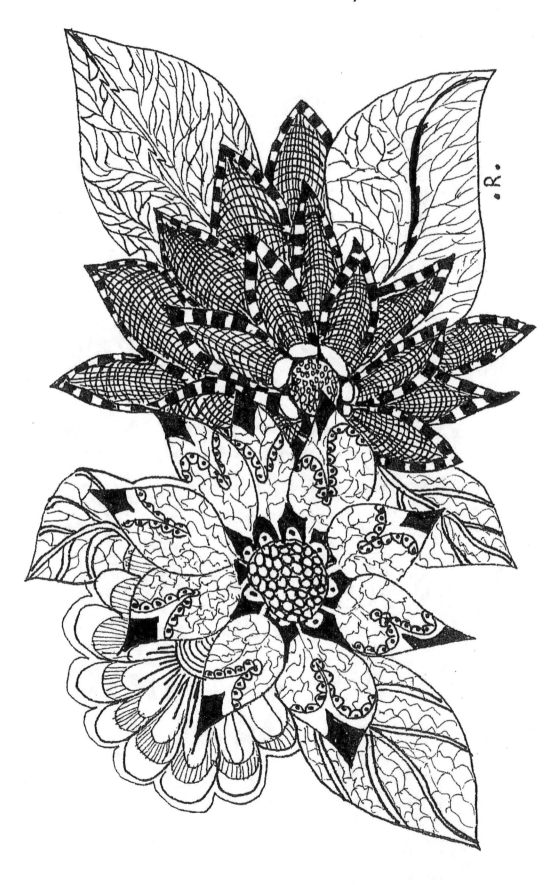

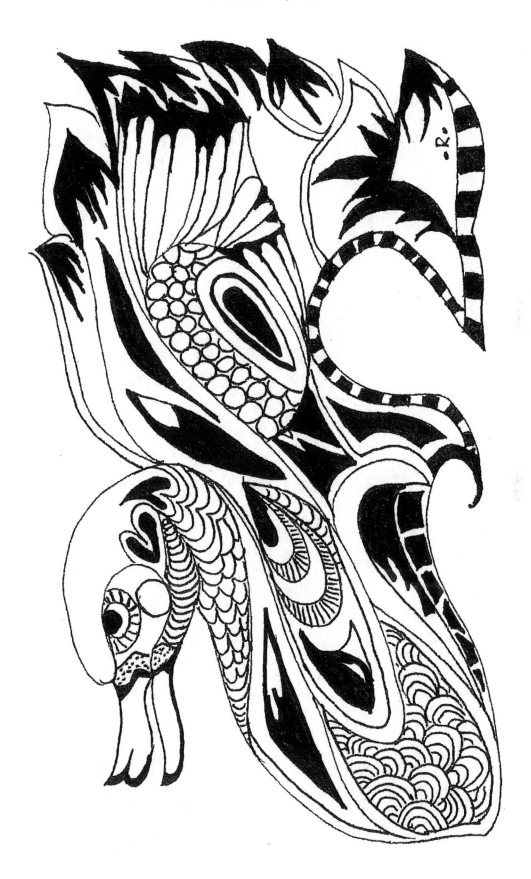

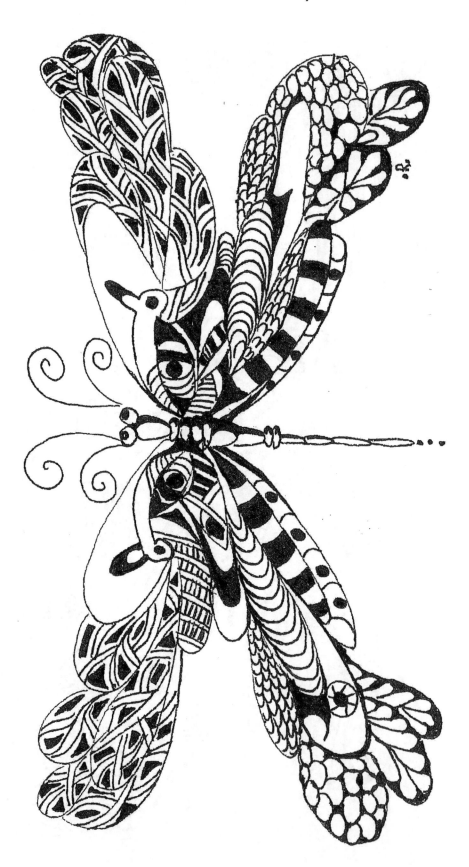

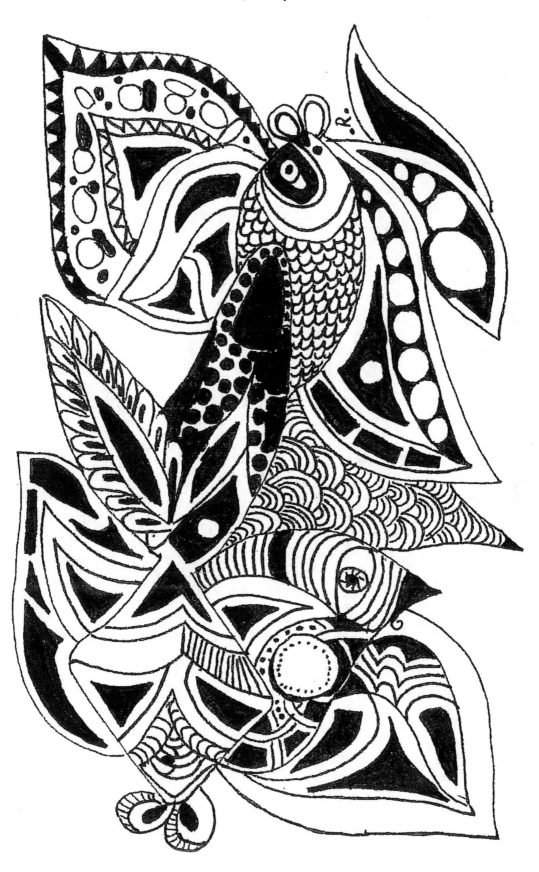

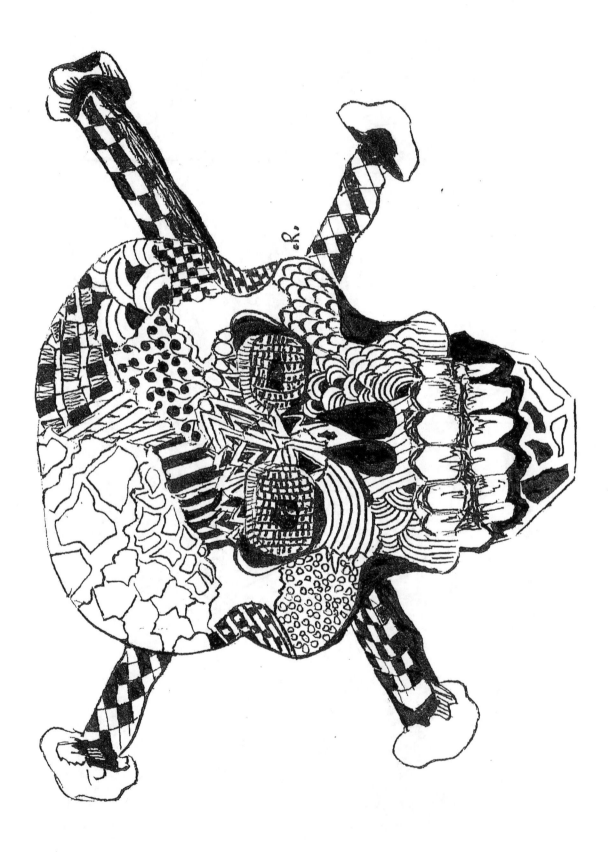

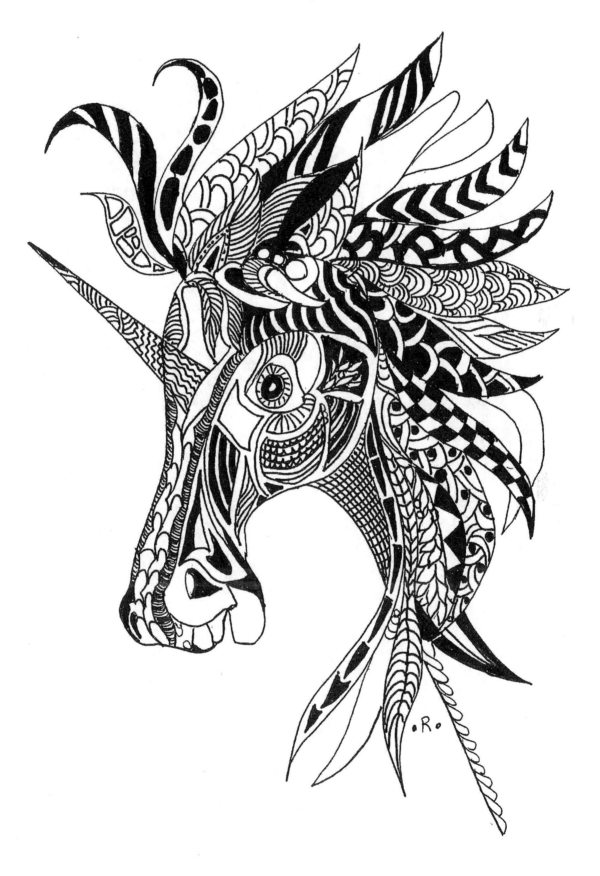

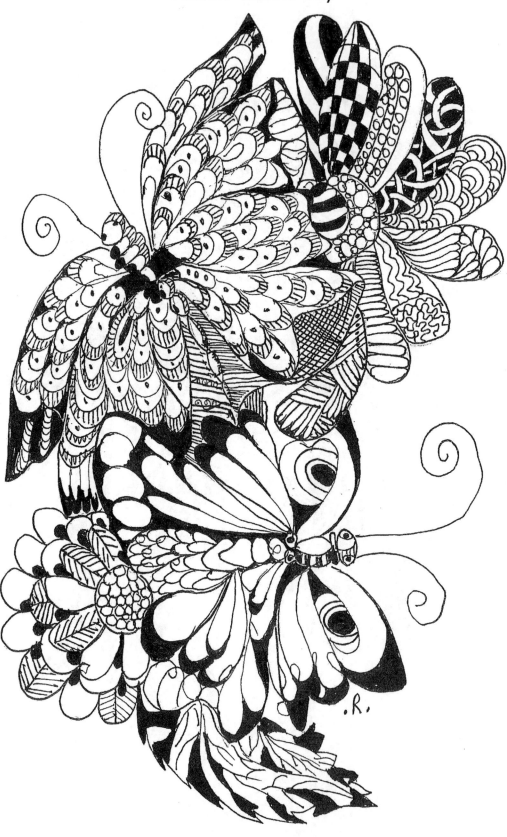

Printed in the United States
By Bookmasters